First-hand Science

Plants and Flowers

Lynn Huggins-Cooper

Illustrated by
Shelagh McNicholas and David Burroughs

A+
Smart Apple Media

First published in 2003 by Franklin Watts
96 Leonard Street, London EC2A 4XD

Franklin Watts Australia
45-51 Huntley Street
Alexandria, NSW 2015

Series editor: Rachel Cooke
Art director: Jonathan Hair
Design: James Marks

Published in the United States by Smart Apple Media
1980 Lookout Drive, North Mankato, Minnesota 56003

Library of Congress Cataloging-in-Publication Data

Huggins-Cooper, Lynn.
Plants and flowers / Lynn Huggins-Cooper ;
illustrated by Shelagh McNicholas and David
Burroughs.
p. cm. — (First-hand science)
"First published in 2003 by Franklin Watts ...
London"—T.p. verso.
Includes index.
Summary: Ruby learns basic facts about plants and
flowers in her aunt's garden.
Contents: Plants everywhere! — Fabulous flowers —
Seeds to grow — Seed to jack-o'-lantern! — Plant food
— By the pond — Falling leaves — Through the year —
Try this yourself — Useful words.
ISBN 1-58340-447-3
1. Plants—Juvenile literature. 2. Flowers—Juvenile
literature. [1. Plants. 2. Flowers.] I. McNicholas,
Shelagh, ill. II. Burroughs, Dave, 1952- ill. III. Title.

QK49.H54 2004
580—dc22   2003058964

9 8 7 6 5 4 3 2 1

Contents

Ruby loves gardening.

Plants everywhere!

Ruby is in her aunt's garden. She loves all the different plants that grow there.

Plants grow everywhere—in gardens, parks, and even through cracks in the pavement!

There are lots of different kinds of plants. Do you recognize any of these?

Moss

Fern

Foxglove

Daisy

Lettuce

Ruby helps her aunt plant some flowers.

Look, Ruby. You can see the roots!

Each part of a plant has a different name.

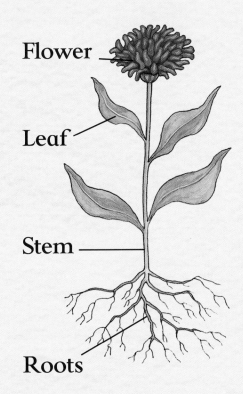

Flower

Leaf

Stem

Roots

???

What's the part of the plant you can't usually see?

It's been a long, hot summer. Some of the plants look droopy and need a drink. Ruby waters them with her can.

Most plants need light to grow.

They also need water.

What do you think happens to a plant if it doesn't get enough water?

Plants cannot run around and collect food!

They use the energy from sunlight to make their own food.

There is special green coloring inside plants which makes food when the sun shines on it. That's why most plants are green!

Ruby loves watching the sunlight shining through the leaves of the trees.

How do we get our food? Why do you think we eat plants?

Fabulous flowers

Ruby sniffs some flowers. They smell like perfume— but the pollen makes her sneeze!

Flowers make **pollen**. You can often see it inside them.

Pollen is powdery, like flour. Sometimes it is bright orange.

Some people are allergic to pollen in the air and get hay fever. This makes their eyes sore and they often sneeze.

Ruby watches fuzzy bumblebees buzzing from flower to flower.

Pollen needs to travel from one flower to another for a plant to make its **fruit**. Insects and the wind help this happen.

Insects like to drink the sweet **nectar** made in flowers—and pollen sticks to them.

When they visit the next flower, they drop some pollen in it.

Grass has feathery flowers. How do you think this helps spread pollen on the wind?

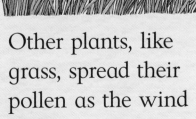

Other plants, like grass, spread their pollen as the wind blows.

Ruby is collecting some juicy fruit in her basket. She has picked blackberries, apples, and plums.

Once pollen has been moved to a flower, its fruit begins to grow. This is how an apple grows each year:

1. Apple flowers are called blossoms. They grow in spring. Insects take pollen from one blossom to another.

What sort of fruit do you like to eat?

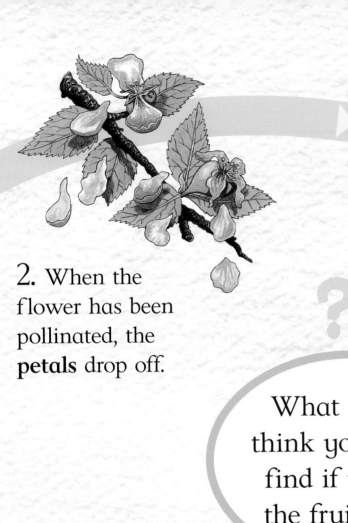

2. When the flower has been pollinated, the **petals** drop off.

3. A tiny green fruit starts to grow.

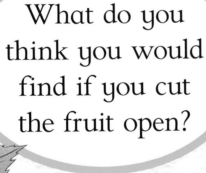

What do you think you would find if you cut the fruit open?

5. The sun shines on the apple and ripens it. By late summer, the apple is ready to eat!

4. Through the summer, the apple grows bigger and bigger.

Seeds to grow

Ruby has eaten an apple. Inside it she has found the small brown pips. A pip is a type of seed.

> If you plant that seed, it will grow into an apple tree.

A **seed** is a package that contains a root and a **shoot**. A new plant will grow from it.

When the seed is planted, the root grows first.

The shoot grows up into the light. The first leaves unfold.

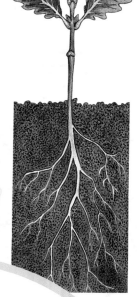

Seeds are found inside fruit. They can be small like an apple pip—or big, like the stone inside a peach or plum.

Ruby and her aunt go on a hunt for other seeds to grow into new plants.

Seeds come in all shapes and sizes.

Kidney beans

Sunflower seeds

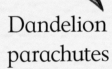
Poppy seeds

Horse chestnuts

Dandelion parachutes

Cherry stones

Seeds have food in them for the new plant. That's why people—and other animals—like to eat them.

Ruby has found burrs stuck to her socks! They hold on with tiny hooks. She picks them off carefully.

Plants need to spread their seeds so they can grow properly. They do this in many ways.

Some seeds catch in the fur of animals so they are carried away.

Some seeds are spread by birds when they eat the fruit—and then "plop" out the seeds.

Ruby scatters the seeds from the burrs. Next year, they will grow into burdock plants.

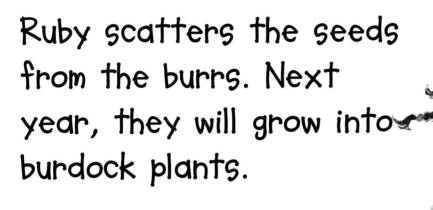

Many seeds lie in the ground through winter. They start to grow when spring comes.

Some seeds are spread by the wind.

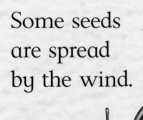

Some seeds are spread when a pod explodes and flings its seeds away.

Some seeds float away on the water.

Seed to jack-o'-lantern!

Ruby and her aunt planted a pumpkin seed in the spring. The tiny seed grew into a big pumpkin plant. There will be pumpkins for Halloween!

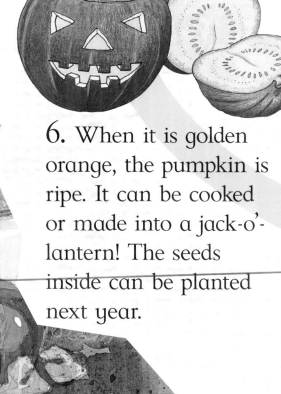

1. This is a pumpkin seed. The root grows first, down into the soil.

6. When it is golden orange, the pumpkin is ripe. It can be cooked or made into a jack-o'-lantern! The seeds inside can be planted next year.

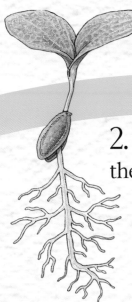

2. Then the stem and the first leaves grow.

Whichever way you plant a seed, the root will grow down and the stem will grow up.

3. When the plant is big, flowers grow. Insects pollinate them.

4. Once a flower is pollinated, the pumpkin fruit starts to grow. The petals die away.

5. The pumpkin grows and swells. It changes color from green to orange.

We eat different parts of different plants. Here are a few:

Leaves: lettuce, cabbage, basil

Stems: rhubarb, chard, celery

Roots: carrots, turnips, beets

Flowers: cauliflower, broccoli

Fruits: strawberries, apples, tomatoes, cucumbers

Plant food

Ruby leaves her pumpkins to grow even bigger. But there are other fruits and vegetables to be picked— and eaten!

Have you eaten any roots, leaves, stems, or flowers today?

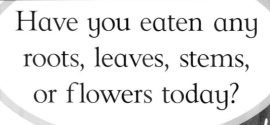

Plants use the energy from sunlight to make food.

Animals eat
the plants

and are eaten by
other animals.

We call this a
food chain.

All food chains
start with a plant.

A snail has already been nibbling this cabbage!

By the pond

Ruby's aunt has a pond in her garden. Lots of plants grow around the pond—and even in the water!

Never go near the pond without me, Ruby! You might fall in!

Water lilies have long stems so their leaves can float on top of the pond while their roots are buried at its bottom.

Some plants grow beside ponds because they like damp soil.

Rushes

Iris

Others grow in the water!

Water lily

Marsh marigold

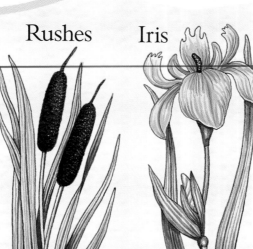

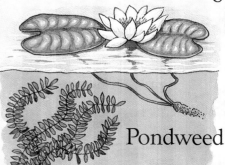

Pondweed

22

Ruby hears plopping sounds. She sees lots of frogs jumping in the water! They find plenty of food by the pond.

Here is a pond food chain.

A water lily uses the energy from sunlight to make food.

A caterpillar eats its leaves.

The caterpillar becomes a moth— and is eaten by a frog.

How is this food chain like the one on page 21?

Falling leaves

Ruby has seen some beautiful red leaves falling onto the pond. The season is changing from summer to autumn.

In autumn, the leaves of many trees change color. Then they fall off. The trees grow new leaves in the spring.

Some trees stay green all year. They are called "evergreens." Christmas trees are evergreens.

What colors do you think of when you think about autumn?

The wind has blown some leaves into a pile. Ruby crunches through them and kicks them into the air!

You can find interesting things in piles of fallen leaves! Here are a few:

Spangle galls

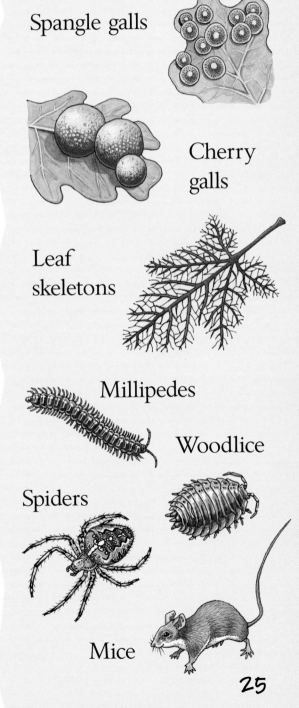

Cherry galls

Leaf skeletons

Millipedes

Woodlice

Spiders

Mice

Through the year

Ruby has collected a lovely harvest to take home. What will she find in the garden on her next visit?

What season do you think it is in each photo? Why?

Find these plants in the pictures. What season do you think of when you see the different plants?

 Poppy

Rose

Pumpkin

Holly

Christmas tree

Daffodil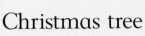

Maple tree with red leaves

27

Try this yourself

Have some plant fun!

Flower "shuteye"

Did you know that the daisies that grow in the grass close up at night? That's how they got their name: "day's-eye." Test this by covering a daisy with a flowerpot for a couple hours. Come back later and see if it has shut!

Mixing seasonal colors

In any season, go for a walk outside and look at all the plants, trees, and flowers. When you get back, take some paints and mix up some seasonal colors for the things you saw. What colors do you think you might use in each season?

Make a leaf "stained-glass window"

Collect a bag of colorful autumn leaves. Tape them to the window with clear tape. As the sun shines through them, you will have a beautiful stained-glass window!

Change color!

See how plants suck up water with this experiment —and change the plants' color, too! Put some water in a jar and add a few drops of red or blue food coloring. Then stand some white flowers (for example, daisies or carnations) in

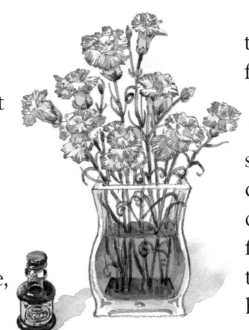

the water. Leave them for a few days—and see some color changes! Try this with vegetables such as celery or cauliflower, too. Ask an adult to cut them open for you after a few days to see how the color has spread.

Useful words

flower: The part of a plant where its fruit and seeds are made.

food chain: A group of plants and animals linked together because one eats another.

fruit: A fruit holds and protects a plant's seeds.

leaf: The part of a plant that makes food using energy from the sun. Leaves are usually green.

nectar: Sweet, sugary liquid made by flowers. It attracts insects, as they like to drink it!

petals: The colorful, leafy parts of a flower.

pollen: Powdery grains made by plants in their flowers. Insects or the wind carry pollen from one flower to another. This pollinates the plant so its seeds can form.

roots: The parts of a plant that grow down into the soil, holding it in place and taking up water.

seed: New plants grow from seeds. A seed contains a root and shoot.

shoot: The tiny stem and leaves that grow up from a seed.

stem: The part of a plant that joins its roots to its leaves and flowers.

About this book

This book encourages children to explore and discover science in their local, familiar environment—in the garden or at the park. By starting from "where they are," it aims to increase children's knowledge and understanding of the world around them, encouraging them to examine objects and living things closely and from a more scientific perspective.

Flowering plants are explored, focusing on their different parts and how seeds are made and grow. Questions are asked to build on children's natural curiosity and encourage them to think about what they are reading. Some questions send children back to the book to find the answers, others point to new ideas that, through discussion, the readers may "discover" for themselves.

Index